The Holy Spirit – Living God

The Holy Spirit – Living God

A biblical, practical and simple guide to the Holy Spirit

Oliver Rice

Grace Publications

GRACE PUBLICATIONS TRUST
7 Arlington Way
London EC1R 1XA
England
e-mail: editors@gracepublications.co.uk
www.gracepublications.co.uk

Managing Editor:
M. J. Adams

© Grace Publications Trust

First published 2011
Reprinted 2021

ISBN 978-0-946462-84-1

Unless otherwise indicated Scripture quotations are taken from the HOLY BIBLE, NEW INTERNATIONAL VERSION. Copyright © 1973, 1978, 1984 by International Bible Society. Used by permission of Hodder & Stoughton, a member of the Hodder Headline Group. All rights reserved.

Printed by Ashford Colour Press, Gosport

Contents

Introduction		7
1.	The Person	9
2.	The Lord God	15
3.	The Author	23
4.	The Enlightener	27
5.	The Life-Giver	33
6.	The Love-Giver	39
7.	The Purifier	51
8.	The Power Source	57
9.	The Gift-Giver	63
10.	The Guarantee	69
Appendix: John Calvin, the theologian of the Holy Spirit		77

Introduction

All Christians need a clear understanding of the Holy Spirit – who he is and what he does – because without the Holy Spirit there could be no Christians and no Christian life.

The aim of this short book is to make these things as clear as possible for 21st century people to understand and use.

> '...how much more will your Father in heaven give the Holy Spirit to those who ask him!' (Luke 11:13)

> 'Be filled with the Spirit'
> (Eph. 5:18)

References in the form (Inst. 1.13.2) show the book, chapter and section number of a quotation taken from John Calvin's major work, *The Institutes of the Christian Religion* (McNeill edition, The Westminster Press, Philadelphia, 1967).

1

The Person

Some people think of the Holy Spirit as no more than a power or force – a kind of divine electricity.

There's a good – but sad – example of this in the Bible (in Acts 8:9-25). A man called Simon, a magician, was impressed by the miracles he saw Philip doing in the name of Jesus by the power of the Holy Spirit. Later, when the apostles Peter and John arrived in the same place, he was impressed by their ability to give the Holy Spirit to the new Christians.

He wanted the same power for himself because he was a man impressed by power. In fact, the people had given him a nickname: 'the Great Power'. But what he saw Peter doing was so much more impressive than anything he could do himself. He therefore asked Peter for the ability to give the Holy Spirit to others and he was prepared to pay for it.

But Peter was not impressed with Simon and this was his response: 'Your heart is not right before God. Repent of this wickedness and pray to the Lord. Perhaps he will forgive you for having such a thought in your heart. For I see that you are full of bitterness and captive to sin' (Acts 8:21-23).

Simon's heart was not right with God nor was his mind clear about the Holy Spirit. The power of the Holy Spirit cannot be bought, and the Holy Spirit is more than mere power.

It is, of course, true that the Holy Spirit is powerful. In fact he is all-powerful ('almighty') because he is God.

It is also true that the Holy Spirit is often associated in the Bible with the power of God – for example, in the book of Judges in the Old Testament or in the book of Acts in the New Testament.

And again, it is the Holy Spirit who gives people the power of God in their lives – as Jesus promised his disciples: 'You will receive power when the Holy Spirit comes on you' (Acts 1:8). (In this respect, chapter 8 of this book looks at the Holy Spirit as our Power Source.)

But the Holy Spirit is not mere Power. He is first and foremost a Person.

The Bible shows this clearly...

Jesus himself always referred to the Holy Spirit as 'he' not 'it' – for example in John 16:14, 'He [the Holy Spirit] will bring glory to me [Jesus]', and throughout John chapters 14-16.

He also called the Holy Spirit the 'counsellor' – or 'comforter', or 'helper'. These words translate a very rich word in the language in which the New Testament was originally written (Greek): 'The Counsellor or Paraclete, from the Greek word "parakletos" (meaning one who gives support), is a helper, adviser, strengthener, encourager, ally, and advocate' (Packer, CT, p.143).

In fact, Jesus promised that the Holy Spirit would be 'another Counsellor' (John 14:16) – to replace himself when he had returned to the Father in heaven. How could 'another Counsellor' be anything other than personal, another person? Even more significantly, this word translated 'another' means 'another of the same kind' (as Jesus) not 'another of a different kind' – which resolves the matter even more certainly. The Holy Spirit is Jesus' replacement helper. We might even say he is Jesus' 'alter ego', his 'other self'. In fact, the Bible can refer to the Holy Spirit as 'the Spirit of Jesus' (Acts 16:7, Phil. 1:19). This is because the Holy Spirit comes from Jesus (his gift to believers) and represents all that Jesus is to us now. It is in fact better for us to have the Holy Spirit here and now than it was for the first disciples to have Jesus in the flesh back then – according to Jesus in John 16:7. If this was a replacement of personal with impersonal, this would make no sense.

It is even better to have the personal Holy Spirit with us and in us than to have the personal Jesus walking and talking alongside us – though, as we have said, what the Holy Spirit does is to bring Jesus closer to us and thus make the relationship more personal.

The Bible also shows us the personal nature of the Holy Spirit in other ways.

Perhaps the most striking example of this appears in Ephesians 4:30 where it is written, 'Do not grieve the Holy Spirit of God.' It is therefore possible to 'grieve' the Holy Spirit – by the way we live and speak. You can make the Holy Spirit sad, you can hurt his feelings. This is not something you can do to a power or a thing. No matter how much you might curse or even kick your computer when it lets you down, you will not hurt its feelings. It has no feelings, unlike the Holy Spirit who is a person.

In addition, there are many other indications in the Bible that the Holy Spirit is a thinking, speaking, choosing, feeling – and therefore, *personal* – being.

Without question the Bible in general, and Jesus Christ in particular, present the Holy Spirit as a person.

Action points

➤ When you talk about the Holy Spirit, talk about him in personal terms – 'he', not 'it'. Otherwise you surely dishonour him, as you would dishonour any person by speaking of them impersonally. (It is not that unusual for Christians to fall into the tendency of speaking and thinking of the Holy Spirit as more of a power than a person – in essence, to forget that Christianity is a relationship, not merely a source of strength.)

➤ Relate to the Holy Spirit as a person, not as a power. When we 'relate' to a television, for example, we obviously relate to a power – which we can control, switch on and off, change channel etc. It is quite acceptable (even necessary) to control a power, but we should not try to control a person, especially a divine person. In fact, if we are wise we will want the Holy Spirit to 'control' or 'fill' us, because 'the mind controlled by the Spirit is life and peace' (Rom. 8:6) and 'where the Spirit of the Lord is, there is freedom' (2 Cor. 3:17). This is to say, if we are wise, we will want the Holy Spirit to be the major influence in our lives and on our minds, for this will mean for us spiritual life, peace and freedom.

➤ Remember that you can grieve the personal Holy Spirit by the way you live, speak and think (Eph. 4:30 and surrounding verses). 'Get rid of all bitterness, rage and anger...' (Eph. 4:31). Alternatively and positively, you can choose to please the Holy Spirit, to make him glad. It's a personal relationship. 'Be kind and compassionate to one another, forgiving each other...' (Eph. 4:32). This is good for all your relationships – with other people and with the Holy Spirit. As you can see, the Holy Spirit should directly affect our relationships with other people.

➤ 'Be very careful, then, how you live' (Eph. 5:15). The word translated 'live' here can also be translated 'walk', as in our daily walk of life. You may remember, as a child, playing 'don't step on the cracks of the pavement' as you walked down the street. You had to be very careful where you stepped or how you walked. The Bible tells us to live with the same kind of care and attention, particularly as we face the challenges and temptations of life. Otherwise, we run the risk of grieving the Holy Spirit and quenching his power within us.

2
The Lord God

The Holy Spirit is a person, but he is not merely a created person like a human or an angel, even a super-angel (or 'archangel').

The Holy Spirit is the Lord God himself.

He is the third person of what Christians refer to as the Trinity – God the Father, God the Son and God the Holy Spirit.

He is equal with the Father and the Son – third in the traditional 'order' perhaps (Father, Son and Spirit) – but not third in importance or status.

Again, it is not difficult to confirm this from the Bible…

First of all, Jesus said that baptism takes place 'in the name of the Father and of the Son and of the Holy Spirit' (Matt. 28:19) – not just in the name of God or in the name of Jesus, but in the name of the Trinity, the three-in-one God. The three persons belong together.

Secondly, Paul signs off a letter in the Bible with a prayer for his readers that 'the grace of the Lord Jesus Christ, and the love of God, and the fellowship of the Holy Spirit be with you all' (2 Cor. 13:14).

It is clear from this prayer that the Holy Spirit is on the same level and in the same team or the same family as the Father and the Son. The 16th century Christian writer John Calvin pointed out that we experience the grace of Jesus and the love of God through the fellowship of the Spirit. The three persons and their gifts are interwoven and interdependent. They work together as a team.

If you cut into the heart of the New Testament part of the Bible, you will find that it is deeply 'Trinitarian' (pervaded by the Trinity). Try Romans 8 for a particularly intense experience of how God works as the three-person team of Father, Son (Christ) and Holy Spirit.

God is Father, Son and Holy Spirit – one God in three persons. Sometimes, around Christmas time, we hear Mary, Joseph and Jesus referred to as 'the holy family' but it is much more appropriate to use this expression to refer to God the Father, God the Son and God the Holy Spirit – indeed, the divine family.

One God in three persons: not three gods (sometimes called 'tritheism'), not one Person appearing in three different ways or modes (sometimes called 'modalism') – like the same man can be a father, son and brother. This is a reality much more complex and mysterious. There really are no adequate illustrations or analogies (like a three leaf clover) in the world for the unique Being that is the three-in-one God.

And this is the only God there is. Calvin says that the Trinity marks off the true God from all false gods – that is to say, all false perceptions of God, the myriad of idols which sinful humans love to fashion for themselves.

'God also designates himself by another special mark to distinguish himself more precisely from idols. For he so proclaims himself the sole God as to offer himself to be contemplated clearly in three persons. Unless we grasp these, only the bare and empty name of God flits about in our brains, to the exclusion of the true God' (Inst. 1.13.2).

It is of the very essence of God that he is 'triune', or three-in-one. Any other representation of 'God' is in fact not God at all. In this perspective, the Muslim view of God ('Allah') is not simply slightly different from the Christian view (as some like to say) but fundamentally different. The true God is triune – both one and three – and anything else is an idol, a false god.

Centuries earlier the truth of God's triunity was expressed like this: 'I cannot think of the one without quickly being encircled by the splendour of the three; nor can I discern the three without being immediately carried back to the one'(Inst. 1.13.17).

This, says Calvin, is not only the proper way to think of God, but it gives 'vitality' to the idea of God. The 'livingness' of God is seen in his triunity, in his dynamic, creative and redemptive activity as Father, Son and Holy Spirit.

Moreover, the doctrine of the Trinity is no abstract, lifeless orthodoxy. It is charged with the life-renewing power of God.

'There, indeed, does the [Christian] mind perceive the very presence of God, and almost touches him, when it feels itself quickened, illumined, preserved, justified, and sanctified'(Inst. 1.13.13).

In other words, Calvin is saying that in the doctrine of the Trinity, rightly taught, the living God is present and active. So real is his presence that the believer almost touches God! We not only perceive God as Trinity but we experience God as Trinity – as our Creator, Redeemer and Sanctifier.

This is the powerful 'mystery' of the Trinity. But we must be careful with the word 'mystery'…

When we use the word 'mystery' we do not mean 'mumbo-jumbo' or irrational nonsense. We do not mean something that we cannot understand at all but something that we cannot understand fully (or perhaps anywhere near fully). We mean that the whole thing is just too big for us to completely take in. I remember my two year old daughter entering London's Millennium Dome for the first time. This tiny person in this huge 'tent' just stopped in her tracks, looked up and around and, with wide eyes, exclaimed: 'Wow! Big!' She was overwhelmed by the vastness of it, just as we are before the vast and awesome mystery of the Trinity.

And is it really any wonder that there is mystery here? Should we not expect some mystery with God, particularly when we are talking about God in himself, the very essence of God, the inner life of God? There are times when it seems like we barely understand ourselves in any deep sense, or the other human beings around us, so is it any wonder that we do not fully understand the Supreme Being who is far, far greater than we are?

Therefore, an element (not to say, a large chunk) of mystery is absolutely to be expected in our knowledge of God. The Bible itself (God's revelation in words) teaches us to expect this when it declares that as well as all the revealed things we have from God, there are 'secret things' (Deut. 29:29) that God has not shared with us, which we do not need to know, which may not even be good for us to know (at least for now). Whilst the truth of the Trinity is revealed to us, there is also a sense in which much remains hidden to us, for while we do know the triune God truly (by the revelation we have in Jesus and the Bible) we certainly do not know him fully.

Packer reflects this sense of the bigness of this truth when he writes: 'The historic formulation of the Trinity ... seeks to circumscribe and safeguard this mystery (not explain it; that is beyond us), and it confronts us with perhaps the most difficult thought that the human mind has ever been asked to handle. It is not easy; but it is true.' (Packer, CT, p.40)

This calls for intellectual humility – not easy for our 'scientific' culture.

And yet, we must also say that there is a difference between a mystery (or paradox) and a contradiction. Our understanding of God as Trinity is not a contradiction, because we do not say that God is one in the same way as he is three; we say that he is one *being* (or essence) in three *persons*. This does not dissolve the mystery of the Trinity – indeed it protects the mystery that it must be – but it is not a contradiction.

We are talking about God the Father, God the Son and God the Holy Spirit. They are on the same team, on the same level, in the same family.

The truth of the Trinity is in itself a clear indication that the Holy Spirit is fully God. But we can add more...

For example, the Bible says very clearly that the Holy Spirit has the abilities of God – to be everywhere at once, for example. 'Where can I go from your Spirit? Where can I flee from your presence?' (Ps. 139:7). The implication of this is 'nowhere' – he is inescapable because he is omnipresent!

This ability is obviously something that only God has. Much as we might wish sometimes that we could be in two places at once, this is in God's power alone. Not even the most powerful angels, or the devil himself, however highly mobile they must be, can be in more than one place at once, as far as we know. But the Holy Spirit can be everywhere at the same time (and not just in 'bits' but in his entirety – which is far beyond our grasp).

Hebrews 9:14 calls him 'the eternal Spirit'. Eternality, or everlastingness, is a quality of God alone and not of anything created. It is more than 'immortality' which means that we may now live forever from this point forward. It means that the Holy Spirit has always been and never had a beginning and always will be. With the Father and the Son he is eternal – together they are the eternal Trinity.

The Holy Spirit is also clearly involved in God's work of creation. As early as the second verse of the Bible he is said to be there at the beginning of God's creation of the heavens and the earth. He is no creature; he is the Creator Spirit.

Perhaps the clearest and strongest indication of all that the Holy Spirit is God is found in Acts 5 verses 3 and 4. In verse 3 Peter, one of the first leaders of the church, rebukes a dishonest man with the words: 'You have lied to the Holy Spirit' (another reminder that he is also personal – capable of being lied to). Then (in verse 4) he says: 'you have not lied to men but to God'. So when the man lied to the Holy Spirit, he lied to God. The Holy Spirit is God.

Action points:

➤ Honour (respect, revere) the Holy Spirit as God. He is as important to your life and salvation as the Father and the Son.

➤ Trust and depend on the Holy Spirit as God. The Holy Spirit is everywhere, knows everything and can do anything. Therefore, with the Father and the Son, he is totally deserving of all your worship and all your confidence.

➤ Get excited – and expectant – about the Holy Spirit! He is God 'at work' (Moody). And if you are a Christian, you have the Holy Spirit within you. This means something very exciting. Since the Holy Spirit is God, your potential is unlimited.

> Our potential is not to be measured in terms of our personal character and heredity, our self-discipline, education and upbringing. We are ... figures of unlimited potential. Maybe by disposition and temperament we are weak and inadequate. But... , waiting upon the Lord, we

renew our strength. We mount up, with wings, as eagles. We run and are not weary. We walk and are not faint. We have it in us to be more than conquerors – hyper-conquerors – and may even say with Paul: 'I can do all things through him who strengthens me'. Such a person can endure any pain, bear any burden, climb any mountain, overcome any foe (MacLeod, p.47).

How ridiculous it is when we doubt that he can work in our lives – he is God!

3
The Author

The Bible was a written by over forty (very different) men, but behind them all was the Holy Spirit as the ultimate author.

This is not to say that these men were simply like secretaries taking dictation from the Holy Spirit (as claimed in some religions), because it is clear as you read the Bible that their own humanity, personality and individuality comes through in their writings.

In the Bible, Peter puts it this way: 'Men spoke from God as they were carried along by the Holy Spirit' (2 Peter 1:21).

'Carried along' translates the same word used in Acts 27:15 where a ship was carried along, blown along, or driven along by the wind.

So we could say that these men's minds (and voices and pens) were blown along by the strong breeze of the Holy Spirit, working through their personalities, taking them where the Holy Spirit wanted them to go – making the Holy Spirit the primary author behind the words of the Bible.

The driving force behind the words of the writers of the Bible was the Holy Spirit, not merely human thoughts, ideas or feelings.

Again the Bible says: 'All Scripture [the Bible] is God-breathed [breathed out by God]' (2 Tim. 3:16). It is good to note here that the original (Greek) word used for 'breath' is the same as that for 'spirit' (and 'wind'). It is the Greek word 'pneuma' – which now appears in our English 'pneumatic' (as in 'pneumatic drill' – air-powered drill). So the Bible was God-breathed or God-spirited – produced by the Holy Spirit.

In a similar way, the book of Hebrews in the New Testament (the second part of the Bible) often introduces quotations from the Old Testament (the first part of the Bible) with the words: 'the Spirit says'. In this line of thought, what the Bible says is identical to what the Spirit says. What the Bible says, the Spirit says. The Holy Spirit is the author of the Bible.

This, of course, is the true basis for the Bible's extraordinary unity of thought and themes – behind the human minds involved in its formation (around 40, over a 1500 year period), there lies the one Divine Mind of the Holy Spirit.

From this divine authorship flows the critical importance of the Bible for human life: specifically its authority, truthfulness and supreme usefulness.

The Bible speaks to us with divine authority because it is authored by God the Holy Spirit. We should listen carefully and respond obediently.

The Bible speaks to us truthfully and reliably because it comes from the God 'who cannot lie'. We can follow it confidently.

The Bible speaks to us as the supremely 'useful' book (2 Tim. 3:16) because it comes from the Maker of everything, ourselves included. In this respect, it could be called the Maker's instruction manual – although its style and content is far richer than this alone.

Action points:

> Read the Bible carefully.

In the Bible itself, Peter writes: 'Pay attention to it [the Bible], as to a light shining in a dark place' (2 Peter 1:19). The world may be a dark place, but here is a light to guide us through – 'a lamp to [our] feet and a light for [our] path' (Ps. 119:105).

In other words, since the Bible is God's 'word', it is well worth reading – as one newspaper has advertised itself, it is 'writing worth reading'. More than that, we should 'pay careful attention to it' – involving study and concentration as far as our minds (with God's help) will take us. This will include memorization of key parts of the Bible, meditation on them and focused listening to clear Bible teaching. What could be more important than to 'pay attention' to God's book?

In the 'Peanuts' comic strip, Lucy says to Charlie Brown: 'I just completed a course in speed reading and last night I read "War and Peace" in one hour... it was about Russia'. Speed reading has its place but sometimes we need to slow down to read the Bible deeply.

➤ Use the Bible so that it changes our lives.

In the Bible, Paul tells us to use the Bible to discover salvation through personal trust in and commitment to Jesus Christ, and to equip us for living life God's way (2 Tim. 3:15-17).

So let's use it, remembering that, as someone has put it: 'the Bible that is falling apart (through plenty of use) is read by someone who isn't'.

4
The Enlightener

When I was an advisor for a Bible college, I was sometimes asked to clarify questions students were asked in courses written by people other than myself. I then had to try to figure out what the writer of the question could have meant. It would be much easier if I could have just asked the question-writer directly: 'what do you mean by that?' Sometimes we also struggle to understand the Bible and we want to ask the author: 'what does it mean?'

The good news is that we have that opportunity.

The Holy Spirit not only authored the Bible, he also stands by to help us understand it – not merely on a surface level but deeply – to grasp and appreciate its real meaning, the meaning he intends.

1 Cor. 2:12-14 explains: '[We have received] the Spirit who is from God, that we may understand what God has freely given us ... The man without the Spirit does not accept the things that come from the Spirit of God ... and he cannot understand them, because they are spiritually discerned.'

In other words, only the Holy Spirit can give us the real meaning of his book, the Bible.

Why is this necessary? After all, we can read most books without this kind of divine help. Is it because the Bible is written in a kind of code that needs to be cracked by super-intellectual (or super-spiritual) code-crackers? Not at all! The Bible is written in basically simple and straightforward language that most people can easily understand. It is not a puzzle.

So we do not need the help of the Holy Spirit for a merely intellectual reason. The fact is that we need the enlightenment of the Holy Spirit for a spiritual reason...

Sin, the evil thoughts and desires inside us all, has twisted our minds. More than anything it is a prejudice, or bias, of our minds against God.

The Bible explains it by telling us that people suppress the truth that God reveals (Rom. 1:19).

This makes us unable to really understand what God wants to say to us through the Bible. It's not simply that we can't understand, but that we won't – we really don't want to know about God. The failure to believe is fundamentally a refusal to believe. Even in the face of powerful evidence, we read:

'Even after Jesus had done all these miraculous signs in their presence, they still would not believe in him' (John 12:37).

There is something in all of us that simply does not like being told what to do. Perhaps we sense a surge of that spirit as we listen to a song like Frank Sinatra's keynote song '*My Way*' – I did it my way, nobody else's way, not God's way, and I am defiant to the end, to the 'final curtain'. That may be a moving song but it is a deeply flawed attitude for life, and a truly disastrous attitude to carry into eternity.

The truth is we don't like being told what to do – by bosses, teachers, parents, policemen, the government ... and ultimately, by God himself, the authority above all others, the supreme authority – the Authority who gives authority to all human authorities. We are like the child I saw at a theme park wearing a shirt with the words: 'Do I have to?' You may recognise this attitude inside yourself. It is not only children who think this way.

It is this attitude (basically a rebellious heart) that the Holy Spirit changes, so that we can have the desire and the power to understand what God is saying to us in the Bible. In any classroom, students who want to understand what is being taught will get a lot further than those who simply can't be bothered. To use a slightly dated word, but still a good one, the Holy Spirit makes us 'teachable', able and willing to learn from God.

Some people think (and some academics make out) that understanding the Bible is a terribly complex business that the average person cannot handle. But this is not really true. John Calvin reduced it, very helpfully, to two essentials. In Latin, which I'll use just because the words rhyme and may then be more memorable, they are: '*orare et laborare*'. In English, this simply means: 'prayer and work/study'. If we are prepared to work hard on the Bible, to study it with all our minds, and to ask for and continually depend on the help of the Holy Spirit, we will not go far wrong and we will begin to discover 'wonderful things' in there.

The simplicity of this approach is refreshing and encouraging, improved only by the addition to it of Martin Luther's '*tentatio*' – our experience of life's trials and temptations. In other words, alongside prayer and study, the hard knocks and challenges of life itself (which are all under the providence and control of God) can teach us. As Calvin would say, experience can be our teacher and help us to grasp the meaning of our life-book, the Bible.

Of course, God has given his church human teachers – past and present, alive and dead (yet still speaking through their writings) – and we should not be slow to consult these for guidance, but our primary teacher is the Holy Spirit himself, the very Author of the Bible.

Moreover, Christian life is not a solitary business but a life lived in community or family, the 'family of believers' (Gal. 6:10). And so we rely not merely on the teachers of the church but on each other, all the brothers and sisters in the family, for clearer understanding of God's word in the Bible. This is not merely theoretical but practical experience, because Christians know that we get further together in our grasp of God's truth as we study the Bible together. The Spirit of enlightenment is also the Spirit of love and community.

Action points:

> Whenever you read the Bible, ask the Author (the Holy Spirit) very simply for understanding. Then read prayerfully, consciously depending on him throughout, as though he were by your side, standing by to be your helper – because indeed he is.

Ask him to remove all the roadblocks set up in your mind by sin, the prejudice we find inside ourselves against God and his truth, and create a clear road for right understanding and life-transforming belief. And keep praying and working at the text until this begins to happen. It usually takes time before clarity breaks into our darkened minds.

You could use this prayer from the Bible: 'Open my eyes that I may see wonderful things in your law [the Bible]' (Ps. 119:18).

Pray that the Holy Spirit will produce in your mind, motives and life-style the impact he intended the words to produce, so that you will really hear what God wants to say to you through the Bible.

> Pray and work (*orare et laborare*). Work hard at understanding; love God with all your mind, even as you pray for his enlightenment: 'Reflect … for the Lord will give you insight' (2 Tim. 2:7).

> Regularly talk about the Bible with other Christians, who also have the Holy Spirit within them, and listen keenly to good Bible teaching, especially at church when we

meet together in Jesus' name and expect his presence by the Spirit. 'Let us not give up meeting together ... but let us encourage one another' (Heb. 10:25). This mutual encouragement is not simply a matter of patting one another on the back and telling one another how well we are doing. It is primarily the encouragement of sharing the word of God together (e.g. 1 Thess. 4:18), which is essential to Christian life, particularly in the tough times. (Hebrews was written for Christians being persecuted and tempted to give up on Jesus.) This mutual encouragement with the word of God is also a very good reason to make going to church, and church Bible studies, a regular thing in your life. Nothing encourages us or gives us hope like the word of God in the Bible, especially as we share it together as a good spiritual meal.

5
The Life-Giver

Physical life

Although we have many troubles in this life, life itself is surely a wonderful gift. It is clearly a gift and not a right, for how could anyone earn the right to life before life has even begun? It is a gift that comes from a good and loving God.

In particular, God the Holy Spirit, the third person of the Trinity, is the giver of life. In its early days, the church referred to him in one of its creeds (statements of belief) as 'the Lord and giver of life'. In this respect, we may legitimately call him the Creator Spirit. As early as the second verse of the Bible (Gen. 1:2), the Holy Spirit is said to be active in creation, 'hovering over the waters' like an eagle supervising its young with great concern.

Later in Gen. 2:7 we read this: 'The LORD God formed the man from the dust of the ground and breathed into his nostrils the breath of life, and the man became a living being.'

This verse is talking about the gift of human life at creation – filling with life (physical, spiritual, intellectual) at its very best what was initially formed by God.

Here's another way the Bible puts it: 'The Spirit of God has made me; the breath of the Almighty gives me life' (Job 33:4).

It is good for us to note here that the Hebrew word used in the Old Testament for 'spirit' and 'breath' is the same word.

The breath of God the Holy Spirit is the breath of life itself. Indeed, all life, energy and movement is the gift and inspiration of the Holy Spirit.

'In him we live and move and have our being' (Acts 17:28).

The Holy Spirit is the Spirit of life, the life-giver.

New life

The Holy Spirit is also the giver of what the Bible calls 'new life'. This is necessary because the rich kind of life originally given to humanity was lost through our disobedience to God. It began, as described in Genesis 3, when Adam and Eve disobeyed God's one prohibition and threw away the deeply satisfying life of intimacy with God that had been theirs.

Since then we have needed 'new life' – or 'renewed life' – the renewal of the rich creation life humans once enjoyed and were made for. In his popular book *Mere Christianity*, C.S. Lewis points out that God's purpose through Christ (and the Holy Spirit) is not simply to make us nice people, but to make us new people.

It's not really so hard to be nice. It is socially unacceptable to be nasty, and if we are nice it is likely that people will be nice in return. In addition, all we have to do often to be 'nice' is to be polite and friendly, to say 'Good morning' to our neighbours and so on. 'Niceness' is within the natural power of anyone, but 'newness' is different. To make us new, to really change us, takes supernatural power – the power of the Holy Spirit.

This action of the Holy Spirit is sometimes referred to as 'regeneration'. Talk of 'inner city regeneration' means the radical renewal of run-down, degenerate inner cities. The Holy Spirit specializes in personal, spiritual renewal – inner life renewal, deep within our souls and ourselves. The Bible also refers to God's gift of a 'new heart', where the 'heart' is the control-centre of human personality.

It is a radical thing. So radical that Jesus called it being spiritually 'born again' (John 3). This event changes a person deeply on the inside. It is not simply a cosmetic change ('what not to wear'). It is a little like putting a brand new engine in an old car – without all the grease.

Action points:

➤ Recognise that the life in you is a gift from God the Holy Spirit. Sometimes we behave as if our lives belonged to us, as if we had made ourselves and we are free to do with them, or to end them, as we wish (as in the play 'Whose Life is it Anyway?'). Of course they do not belong to us; they are a gift from God and the answer to the title and theme of that play is: not mine, but God's.

➤ Respect the gift of life, especially human life which is special according to the Bible – God's special creation. Life is not cheap.

(Very briefly: medical ethics, or 'bioethics', can be highly complex, but, in light of creation, doesn't the basic principle have to be 'err on the side of life'?).

➤ According to Jesus Christ: 'You must be born again' (John 3:7). 'Must': if there is one essential in life, this is it. When the powerful preacher, George Whitefield, was asked why he preached so often on the text 'you must be born again', he simply said, 'because you *must* be born again!' In John 3, Jesus went on to say that without this miracle no-one can see or enter the kingdom of God/heaven.

➤ It is thereafter a case of: new life, new lifestyle. A person who has received new spiritual life from the Holy Spirit (through faith in Jesus Christ) must and can begin to live a new lifestyle – the kind detailed in the Bible.

Putting it another way: 'The fruit of the Spirit is love, joy, peace, patience, kindness, goodness, faithfulness, gentleness and self-control' (Gal. 5:22).

Following the new birth (regeneration), this is what the Holy Spirit increasingly produces in a person's life – a new quality and way of life that is beautiful, liberating and totally relevant to everyday life. This is called sanctification.

6
The Love-Giver

God's love

'God has poured his love into our hearts by the Holy Spirit whom he has given us' (Rom. 5:5).

Psychologists (and virtually everyone else on the planet) recognize that the most basic human need is the need to be/feel loved. This, more than anything else, is what makes people feel secure, strong and satisfied.

It is the beautiful and joyful work of the Holy Spirit to fill our hearts with God's love. The great and unique love that comes from God the Father and through his Son our Saviour Jesus Christ (Rom. 5:8) arrives in our hearts and experience by the Holy Spirit.

As Rom. 5:5 (above) celebrates, the Holy Spirit pours God's love into our hearts. Please note that he 'pours' it – extravagantly, generously – because there is so much of it and because he wants us to have so much of it, to be flooded in our inner being with God's love.

Connected with this reality is the reality of our adoption into God's family as his children.

Of all the great things God has done for us, this is surely the greatest. 'Forgiveness' is huge, a huge relief for guilty sinners facing hell and all its misery. 'Justification' is even better – that, through Jesus and through faith in him, God should not only clear our record but positively consider us as right as Jesus himself (which is as right as right can be) – as if we had his record! But 'adoption', that he should also make us his own children, is out of this world. This is grace indeed! As John wrote with enthusiasm: 'How great is the love the Father has lavished on us, that we should be called children of God! And that is what we are!' (1 John 3:1).

Contrary to a very popular idea, all people are not children of God. All people are the creation of God and made in his image but only Christians are children of God in this unique and special way.

In the Bible, John says that whilst many in the world have rejected Jesus Christ (even though he is their creator), 'to all who received him ... he gave the right to become children of God' (John 1:12).

So it is Jesus Christ who makes us God's children (gives us that immense right and privilege), as we receive him by faith as our Saviour and Lord and everything else that he is.

However, it is the Holy Spirit who makes us *feel* that we are God's children.

'The Holy Spirit speaks to us deep in our hearts and tells us that we are God's children' (Rom. 8:16, New Living Translation of the Bible).

He speaks to us deeply or 'testifies with our spirit that we are God's children'.

This deep assurance of God's Father-love is given, at least periodically, to all Christians – all his children – just as any good parent wants his/her children to know/feel on a regular basis that they are loved.

It happens most naturally when Christians draw near to God through Bible study, praise and prayer, whether alone or together with other Christians.

As they seek to connect with God in this way, they may feel very deeply God's Father-love for them personally, as the Holy Spirit works through these channels and 'speaks to us deep in our hearts'.

A good example of this experience is recorded in the Bible in Luke 24:13-32. Two thoroughly dejected followers of Jesus encounter him on the way home from Jerusalem where Jesus has recently been crucified. Intriguingly, they are 'kept from recognising him' (by God, surely) so that Jesus can first show them from the Bible (the Old Testament) that as the promised Messiah he had to suffer and rise again. Basically, he gives them a long Bible study. Are they bored or switched-off? Not at all! Later, they say to one another: 'Were not our hearts burning within us while he talked with us on the road?' They were energized and reinvigorated by the experience and even able to run the seven miles all the way back to Jerusalem to tell other disciples that they had seen and met the risen Jesus.

John Wesley put it in similar words hundreds of years later, whilst listening to biblical truth about Jesus Christ: 'I felt my heart strangely warmed.' As he, and the Emmaus believers, and countless other believers heard and thought through the biblical words and truths, they experienced the heart-warming love of God given by the Holy Spirit.

This special experience is known, at one time or another, to every child of God. This experience also often happens when Christians are suffering, which is where the thought flows in Romans 8. Suffering, in the Christian life, is often also a time of grace, a deeper experience of God's goodness. It can be a real blessing in disguise. It is the experience of God's love in the heart and it makes us want to cry out: 'Father!' as both a cry for help and an expression of trust and dependence.

Indeed, it is a wonderful thing simply to cry to God from the heart with the word: 'Father!' Martin Luther felt this and wrote:

> This is indeed a very short word, but it includes everything. Not the lips but the feelings are speaking here, as though one were to say: 'Even though I am surrounded by anxieties and seem to be deserted and banished from your presence, nevertheless I am a child of God on account of Christ; I am beloved on account of the Beloved!' Therefore the term

> 'Father', when spoken meaningfully in the heart, is an eloquence ... the most eloquent of men there have been in the world cannot attain. For this is a matter that is expressed, not in words but in sighs, which are not articulated in all the words of all the orators; for they are too deep for words (Luther's works, Vol. 26, Lectures on Galatians).

Martin Luther wrote these words in response to what he read in the Bible in Galatians 4:6: 'Because you are sons, God sent the Spirit of his Son into our hearts, the Spirit who calls out "*Abba*, Father".' This deep sense of the Father and his love is inspired by the Holy Spirit within us, the Spirit of sonship, who calls out in and through us 'Abba, Father!'

The word 'Abba' deserves more attention – not as a Swedish pop group from the 1970s but as an intimate Jewish family expression. It was, and still is, used by Jewish children to address their father – and it appears to be not unlike a small child's 'dadda' or 'papa'.

James Boice explains it this way:

> When Jesus addressed God as Father he did not use the normal word for father. He used the Aramaic word 'abba'. Obviously this was so striking to the disciples that they remembered it in its Aramaic form and repeated it in Aramaic even in their Greek gospels and other writings... Mk 14:36, Rom 8:15, Gal 4:6... 'abba' was the address of small children to their fathers... 'abba' means 'daddy'. To the Jewish mind a prayer addressing God as daddy would not only have been improper, it would have

> been irreverent to the highest degree. Yet this is what Jesus said, and this quite naturally stuck in the minds of the disciples... It was something quite new and unique when Jesus instructed his disciples to call God daddy (Boice, p.447).

There is some debate as to whether 'abba' is exactly equivalent to 'daddy', yet there is no doubt that it carries a warm sense of family intimacy and affection.

Of course, such an expression does not necessarily imply a childish faith or lack of respect for God. My children still call me 'Daddy' from time to time and I do not normally take it as a sign of disrespect or 'over-familiarity'.

Whilst we do not wish to encourage an infantile faith or a childish approach to life, it is forever true that before our Father God we are only little children – and, like little children, depend entirely upon him. In this sense, Jesus urges us (emphatically) to ask the Father again and again for whatever we think we need, with this confidence: 'how much more [than an earthly human father] will your Father in heaven give good gifts to those who ask him!' (Matt. 7:11).

'Abba' implies both affection and respect, as is entirely appropriate in our relationship with the God who made the world and everything in it. If we do not feel it is appropriate to call God 'Daddy' exactly, we are certainly at liberty to call him 'Abba, Father', as is entirely natural for the children of God. Some suggest 'Dear Father' as most appropriate.

> Although he may be broken and bruised, tossed about with fears and doubts, the child of God

nevertheless in his need cries out, 'Father!' as instinctively as a child who has fallen and been hurt calls out in similar language, 'Daddy, help me!' Assurance of sonship is not reserved for the highly sanctified Christian; it is the birthright of even the weakest and most oppressed believer. This is its glory (Ferguson, pp.184-5).

When we pray, we 'normally' pray to the Father (our 'Abba') through Christ (the Son) and by the Holy Spirit. It is not wrong to pray to the Son or the Spirit direct, for they are fully God and such prayers are found in the Bible (particularly in the gospels); but the 'normal' or 'natural' approach is to the Father, through the Son and by the Spirit, which mirrors in reverse the movement of grace that comes to us from the Father, through the Son and by the Spirit.

'For through him [Christ] we ... have access to the Father by one Spirit' (Eph. 2:18). The whole Trinity may be involved as we pray and we are caught up in the flow (and overflow) of the divine love – for, of course, both the movement from above and the movement from below are orchestrated by grace because even our response to God is motivated by God the Holy Spirit who creates faith and inspires prayer.

This makes prayer as much (perhaps more) a gift than a duty, and positions the Holy Spirit as 'God on our side of the relationship' (Smail, p.205).

Family love

Alongside this enriching experience of the Father's love we

may place the enriching experience of the family's love – the love of the Christian family. Of course, since 'love comes from God' (1 John 4:7) as its true source, this is also an expression of the Father's love through the family.

God has no 'only children' and should have no 'lonely children'. 'God sets the lonely in families' (Ps. 68:6), above all in the 'family of believers' (Gal. 6:10). And the family of God depends completely for its 'life of love' (Eph. 5:2) on the Holy Spirit, the love-giver (Rom. 5:5).

On this foundation, the Bible tells Christians to 'keep the unity of the Spirit through the bond of peace' (Eph. 4:3). From this it is clear that the Spirit gives the loving unity (through connection to Jesus Christ) and we are only to 'keep' (not create) it. It cannot be created artificially, merely humanly. The glue is divine, the glue of the Holy Spirit.

In fact, relationships of the highest quality are now possible through Jesus Christ and by the Holy Spirit. For the Holy Spirit produces in people's lives the supreme qualities for good relationships, like: 'love, joy, peace, patience, kindness, goodness, faithfulness, gentleness and self-control' (Gal. 5:22-23).

Significantly, 'love' heads up this list. We know that 'God is love' and that his uniquely deep love has been demonstrated in his Son, Jesus, who died for us while we were still sinners and indeed enemies of God. So it is no surprise that this, above all, is what the Holy Spirit pours into our lives – real, practical love. The other qualities are equally exciting.

Now just imagine your relationships enhanced by these

qualities... And see how very practical and relevant they are for everyday life. On which day do you *not* need patience, for example? What relationship is *not* enriched by kindness and faithfulness? What wouldn't you give for authentic joy and peace in your mind and life? There are many occasions when self-control could make all the difference and save us from foolish and hurtful words and actions; 'Like a city whose walls are broken down is a man who lacks self-control' (Prov. 25:28).

This is the exciting potential for every Christian (and every church) filled with the Holy Spirit.

Of course, realistically no one this side of heaven achieves the full potential of the Holy Spirit, and so there remains conflicts and hurts even amongst Christians. Even so, Christian relationships can be, should be, and often are amongst the very best you can find in this world – due once again to the Holy Spirit, the love-giver.

So the Holy Spirit does not only operate in a personal, spiritual realm – just inside individuals in mystical ways. He also has a powerful social influence, creating God's new society, the church. He is the Spirit of love, of community, the go-between. First of all and above all, the fruit he produces is the good fruit of love (Gal. 5:22).

We can see how the Holy Spirit is the facilitator both of our experience of God's love – as it comes down to us through Jesus Christ, and of our expression of it – as it goes out from us to others. He brings down to earth God's love in Jesus Christ in the Christian community or family. 'No-one has ever seen God; but if we love one another, God lives in us and his love is made complete in us' (1 John 4:12) and, we could add, 'visible in (and amongst) us'. In other words, people should be able to see (and taste) the love of God alive and well in the family of God, the church.

And this love (from God and his people) gives us the support, security and satisfaction we crave. 'Satisfy us in the morning with your unfailing love, that we may sing for joy and be glad all our days' (Ps. 90:14).

The Spirit who connects us to Christ by faith thereby also connects us to one another in love, rather like spokes in the hub of a wheel, and so begins a revolution in our relationships. Reconciliation is the wonderful work of God through Jesus Christ and by the Holy Spirit – peace with God and with one another.

Action points:

➤ If you have received Jesus Christ into your life as your leader and liberator, thank God for your adoption into his family. It is the best thing of all about being a Christian.

Thank him for every experience of his Fatherly and family love.

➤ Give Bible reading, praise and prayer (individually and with Christian brothers and sisters) an absolutely central place in your life, so that you may maintain and deepen your experience of God's love.

➤ Attend a Bible-centred church, where the Bible is read and explained at the heart of the meeting, and where Communion (taking bread and wine in remembrance of Jesus) takes place regularly. Communion matters because it is given by Jesus and it is a simple but effective way to remember him and his sacrifice of love for us together. Moreover, it is (rightly done) an occasion interpreted and enriched by appropriate Bible readings to focus the mind and heart on Jesus.

- 'Make every effort to keep the unity of the Spirit through the bond of peace' (Eph. 4:3). It's not always easy – Christians are a diverse group, with different personalities, ideas and opinions. But we need to work hard at it and in prayerful dependence on the Holy Spirit. 'If it is possible, as far as it depends on you, live at peace with everyone' (Rom. 12:18).

- Be a good Christian brother or sister.

As the Bible puts it: 'as we have opportunity, let us do good to all people, especially to those who belong to the family of believers' (Gal. 6:10). Or, even more challengingly, 'live a life of love, just as Christ loved us and gave himself up for us' (Eph. 5:2). That's a very high standard but it's what God calls us to, and we have the Holy Spirit (the all-powerful Creator!) to help us.

Express and spread the love God has given you through Jesus and the Holy Spirit. This is what should define a Christian and a church more than anything else and make God's love visible to the world around. 'And now these three remain: faith, hope and love. But the greatest of these is love' (1 Cor. 13:13).

7
The Purifier

We hear a lot nowadays about air/water pollution and air/water purification. These are important to our physical health but even more important is spiritual purification, which is vital to our spiritual health and well-being. And this is the business of the Holy Spirit.

In two places in the Bible he is called 'the good Spirit' but most frequently he is called the 'Holy Spirit'. This is surely because his nature is holy (pure) and also because his work is holy. He is holy and he makes people holy. He is holy by name, by nature and by action.

In the Bible, we read about 'the sanctifying [purifying] work of the Spirit' (1 Peter 1:2).

He purifies people from sin – in thought, imagination, desires and lifestyle – just as a breeze of wind can clear and purify the air.

Our minds are deeply infected with sin. It is the job of the Holy Spirit to make personally effective for us and in us the sacrifice of Jesus Christ on the cross to forgive and purify us.

We are purified by the sacrifice of Christ, but as with all Christ's gifts, this takes place by the Spirit. It was by the Spirit that Jesus offered himself sacrificially on the cross (Heb. 9:14) and it is by the Spirit that we receive the power of that sacrifice.

On this basis, the Bible promises us that: 'if we confess our sins, [God] is faithful and just and will forgive us our sins and purify us from all unrighteousness' (1 John 1:9).

How is he 'faithful'? He is faithful to his promise and commitment to forgive through Jesus.

How is he 'just'? He is 'just' (right to forgive) in that through Jesus our guilty sins have already been paid for, so free forgiveness is now a possibility – a reality! – for all who freely confess their sins to God.

This process begins the moment someone becomes a Christian, and continues throughout the Christian life – as we need God's forgiveness and purification every day. Just as we need to wash our hands regularly every day as they get dirty, so we need to confess our sins regularly every day as spiritually our hands get dirty. In this way we also 'keep short accounts with God' (Packer) and maintain a good and close relationship with him.

So the spiritual purification process, through Christ and by the Spirit, takes place on our side through personal confession of sin, the honest admission that we have done specific wrongs in thought, word and action.

Then we must also highlight the vital role played in this process of purification by the Bible – which is, as we considered in chapter 3, the Holy Spirit's book. Here the Holy Spirit uses the Bible to renew our minds.

Jesus made this clear when he prayed for his followers: 'Sanctify [purify] them by the truth; your word [the Bible] is truth' (John 17:17). In other words, Jesus was praying (for us): 'Make my followers holy by applying the truth of the Bible to their minds, hearts and lives.'

The Holy Spirit uses the Bible (his book) to purify our minds and motives. He drives Bible truth deep into our personality, to create within us not merely some new ideas or even new beliefs, but new convictions – new driving-forces at the heart (or control-centre) of our lives...

'Our gospel came to you not simply with words, but also with power, with the Holy Spirit and with *deep conviction*' (1 Thess. 1:5; emphasis added).

When God's message comes to us 'with the Holy Spirit' (with his 'power'), it also comes 'with deep conviction' – and this is what changes and purifies us. He drives into us convictions (like nails deep into wood) that set us free from the control of sin; free to live a new life, free to choose to do the good, right and wise thing.

We can see that the Purifier is also the Liberator – the Spirit who sets us free. 'Where the Spirit of the Lord is, there is freedom' (2 Cor. 3:17; and see also Rom. 8:2). Purity is not a terrible duty laid upon us, taking all the fun out of life. Purification is liberation, a beautiful new freedom from the power and pollution of evil.

And so the Bible directs us to: 'Put into action God's saving work in your lives ... for it is God working in you, giving you the desire to obey him and the power to do what pleases him' (Phil. 2:12-13, New Living Translation).

The Holy Spirit is God at work in us at the deepest level of our lives. Not just at the level of our actions, but at the level of our intentions – our desires and motives. He gives us the 'desire' and the 'power' to obey God and do what pleases him.

In fact, whenever a Christian experiences an impulse to resist the wrong and do the right, we have a right to say that this is evidence of the Holy Spirit at work inside them.

It's like learning to drive with the Holy Spirit as your driving instructor, sitting next to you. You can follow his instructions and drive well, or you can ignore what he says and drive your own way – then lose your way, break down or crash.

Action points:

➤ Regularly confess your sins to God. Wash your spiritual hands every day. Admit your wrongdoing and ask God to strengthen you by his Spirit to turn from it. Confession is indeed good for the soul. It can be a kind of emotional and spiritual respiration where we breathe out our guilt and sin, and we breathe in God's grace and forgiveness.

- Give the Holy Spirit material to work with in your life, mind and motives – namely, the material of his book, the Bible.

'I never saw a useful Christian who was not a student of the Bible. If a person neglects the Bible there is not much for the Holy Spirit to work with. We must have the word' (D.L. Moody).

'I have hidden [or stored up deep] your word in my heart that I might not sin against you' (Ps. 119:11).

This will mean memorizing (storing up) parts of the Bible, key parts, that will serve as motivational material for us in times of trouble or temptation. Spiritually resource yourself in this way; build up your defences; arm yourself against trials that will surely come.

- Work with the Holy Spirit not against him. That is, work with those pure impulses, or recollections of words from the Bible (the Holy Bible), given by the Holy Spirit to help you make good, right and wise choices in everyday life. Resist the impure impulses of your 'sinful nature'. And so develop habits of what the Bible calls 'godliness'.

'Keep in step with the Spirit' (Gal. 5:25).

'Holy Spirit, think through me, till your ideas are my ideas' (Amy Carmichael).

8
The Power Source

After his death and resurrection, Jesus Christ gave his church (Christians) a clear directive: to tell people all over the world all about him.

But he also said that before the first Christians could fulfil this 'mission impossible' they would have to wait for the Father to give them a gift – the gift of the Holy Spirit. This mission cannot be fulfilled by mere human strength or strategy. It is only the Holy Spirit who gives Christians power to fulfil this directive and present Jesus Christ to all kinds of people.

'When the Holy Spirit has come upon you, you will receive power and will tell people about me [Jesus] everywhere' (Acts 1:8; New Living Translation).

More specifically, the Holy Spirit gives Christians the courage for this task. It often requires some courage to tell someone else about Jesus Christ. Some people find it easier than other people, but I'm not sure anyone finds it easy all the time. It often takes courage because there is a basic antagonism in the human mind towards Jesus. It certainly took courage for Peter (in Acts 2) to tell his listeners that the man they had just crucified was no other than their Messiah and Lord. And that courage clearly came to him through the Holy Spirit, not through his own strength or self-confidence.

The Holy Spirit also gives Christians the desire for this task. We may not always feel like it, but when we are filled with the Holy Spirit we are motivated to get on with it. We begin to see it as highly important business, because without Jesus Christ people are lost – for ever. Like the apostle Paul in the Bible we feel like we want to say to our friends: 'I want you to know that through Jesus the forgiveness of sins is proclaimed to you' (Acts 13:38). We want them to know about that more than anything else.

The Holy Spirit gives Christians the words for this, as Jesus promised in Matthew 10:19-20. This is especially true in pressure situations. It does not mean that the Christian need not prepare for such opportunities (because 1 Peter 3:15 says, 'always be prepared to give an answer'), but that in pressure situations like the one described in Matthew, the Holy Spirit will give us the right words to say. And don't forget that he can still work even when we think that our words are muddled and that we have failed!

Finally, the Holy Spirit gives Christians concern for this – that is, concern for other people who do not have Jesus Christ in their lives. In fact, he transmits to us the compassion of Jesus himself who looked on the crowds and saw them 'harassed and helpless, like sheep without a shepherd' (Matt. 9:36).

Action points:

➤ Pray simply:
Lord, please give us the power of your Holy Spirit to present Jesus Christ to our friends, family, neighbours etc. How hard it can be and how easily we become tongue-tied. So please help us Lord!

Remember that regular prayer keeps us connected to the power source. Jesus himself encourages us (over and over again in Luke 11:1-13) to ask, seek and knock for the Holy Spirit, the best of all the Father's gifts to his children: 'how much more will your Father in heaven give the Holy Spirit to those who ask him!' (Luke 11:13).

We must also pray that the Father will give the Holy Spirit to those we talk to about Jesus – because only he can open their understanding, open their hearts, to receive Jesus Christ as Lord and Saviour by faith. 'For God, who said, "Let light shine out of darkness," made his light shine in our hearts to give us the light of the knowledge of the glory of God in the face of Christ' (2 Cor. 4:6).

➤ Don't be afraid or intimidated.

He has promised to be with us – and with us particularly

here, as we present Jesus to people who need him. Remember what 'the great commission' in Matthew 28:18-20 says: 'Go and make disciples ... and surely I am with you always'. It is particularly as we go – to tell others of Jesus, to make them his disciples – that we experience the empowering presence of Jesus Christ by his Spirit.

God's words to Gideon in the book of Judges may also be applied to us: 'Go in the strength you [already] have' (Judg. 6:14) – the strength of the Spirit of the Lord. Gideon was 'simply' (though courageously) to step out in faith, trusting that the strength would be there as he did so (and it was). It is the same for us, and even more so, in our time (in the age of Pentecost and the Holy Spirit).

Not only will he give us the desire for this; he'll also give us the courage and the words to say in pressure situations. So go for it, and trust him to support you.

➤ Jump in!

Don't miss out on this vital aspect of Christian life – your spiritual satisfaction depends on it. When Jesus told his disciples, 'my food is to do the will of him who sent me' (John 4:34), what he meant was this: nothing feeds, nourishes and satisfies my soul more than God's work. It is the same for us as his followers (as you may already have discovered). This is God's work – the business of presenting his message about his Son, Jesus – and it satisfies our souls.

It can be like stepping into the sea – initially freezing, gradually exciting, eventually exhilarating.

What is more, when we get involved in this business (his business), the Holy Spirit gets right behind us, and we experience God's presence and power in a special way (as promised in Matt. 28:18-20).

That is because, when we are declaring the wonderful truths about Jesus we are doing something the Holy Spirit himself loves to do (John 16:14) – and so he 'sponsors' us in this very good cause.

As one Christian has put it, the Holy Spirit 'floodlights' or spotlights Jesus Christ just as important buildings or cathedrals are illuminated to reveal all their glory. We could almost say, he lives to spotlight Jesus Christ, so when we try to do the same, he comes right alongside us to help us.

> He is the <u>hidden floodlight</u> shining on the Saviour, the <u>secret surgeon</u> of the heart who redirects love and desire to the living and true God, and to Jesus in particular, the <u>unnoticed matchmaker</u> who brings us to the feet of Christ, the <u>intercom channel</u> that sustains communication between us and our Lord and the <u>hidden energizer</u> guaranteeing perseverance in faith, hope, love and worship (Packer, in Atkinson, p. 446).

A little boy was asked one Sunday: 'who was your Sunday school teacher?' 'I don't know', he replied, 'but she must have been Jesus' grandmother because she didn't talk about anyone else'. It's the same with the Holy Spirit and it's his intention (and action within us) that it might be the same with us.

Aim to talk about Jesus with someone today.

9
The Gift-Giver

The church is the 'body' or 'team' of Jesus Christ, doing his work on earth and carrying his message and mission to the world.

The Holy Spirit equips this team by giving gifts to the church. He gives all kinds of gifts or abilities, a whole kaleidoscope of them. The church is multi-talented, equipped by God to do his work. Individual believers are to work in their own local church (or sometimes to establish one) and even in the smaller church there is often a rich variety of gifts. Where there are 'gaps', a local church nearby may well be able to fill them.

In this sense, the Holy Spirit could be described as the 'chief administrator' of the church (with Jesus Christ as the 'managing director'). The Holy Spirit distributes abilities (wisely and just as he pleases) to Christians for the effective running of the church as 'the body of Christ'.

The key passage in the Bible to look at is 1 Corinthians 12: 'There are different kinds of gifts, but the same Spirit. There are different kinds of service, but the same Lord. There are different kinds of working, but the same God works all of them in all men' (1 Cor. 12:4-6).

There are disagreements between Christians on this, but it seems clear that a few of the gifts mentioned in this chapter of the Bible ('tongues' and 'prophecy' for example) had only a temporary purpose and duration (for the founding of the church in the world, rather like scaffolding around a building) and are now no longer necessary. These gifts filled out the revelation of the word of God about Jesus Christ and that revelation is now complete in the Bible so that we may be 'thoroughly [or fully] equipped [by it] for every good work' (2 Tim. 3:17). No extra 'revelation' is needed for the Christian life.

However, many gifts of the Holy Spirit remain in operation in the church of Jesus Christ. We may split these into two general categories: speaking gifts (like preaching and Bible teaching) and serving gifts (like administration and encouragement).

We do not need to view the gift lists in the Bible as exhaustive of all the gifts the Holy Spirit makes available to the church. As Calvin happily put it: 'He pours out his gifts, as the sun spreads its beams all over the land' (Commentary on Corinthians). There is virtually an infinite variety, as broad as the gifts and abilities God gives in creation. In fact, since the Holy Spirit is also the Creator Spirit, we have a right to understand the gifts of the Spirit in the church as his gifts of creation renewed and refocused for their true purpose of service to God and others.

The key question is: what are the gifts for? The answer, or answers, can be found in 1 Corinthians 12:

- They are for the glory or praise of Jesus Christ (v3) because it is only by the Holy Spirit that we can say, and really mean, 'Jesus is Lord'. As we saw in chapter 6, all Holy Spirit work aims at this (John 16:14).

- They are for the good of the church (v7 'for the common good') – that means, for the good of each person in the church, including, and even especially, the least prominent or 'important' people who are like parts of the body that deserve special honour (v23) and treatment (v24).

In fact, all genuine Holy Spirit work has this double-aim: the glory of Jesus and the good of others. Such aims should be the chief concern of every individual Christian (Matt. 22:37-40).

And so, any church or Christian group or movement can be effectively evaluated with this question: does it lift up the name of Jesus? If it does, that is the sign of a Spirit-filled (i.e. authentic) church. And secondly, does it display the love of Christ in its social life where people are using gifts and working towards 'the common good'? A love that is focussed on 'the least of these brothers of mine', as Jesus himself expressed it in Matthew 25. For these are both clear marks of a church where the Holy Spirit lives, works and rules.

In fact, in the very next chapter of this biblical letter (1 Corinthians), we are told that the gifts of the Spirit must be controlled by the love of the Spirit. Greater than any ability or action, however spectacular or impressive or even sacrificial, are the beautiful qualities of faith, hope and love, 'and the greatest of these is love' (1 Cor. 13). There is nothing as important as love and no clearer mark of real Spirit-filled Christianity.

You may have noticed that this part of the Bible (1 Corinthians 13) is a big favourite at weddings, but it is important to realise that it is not just for weddings or marriages and it is not just about romantic love.

> Love is patient, love is kind. It does not envy, it does not boast, it is not proud. It is not rude, it is not self-seeking, it is not easily angered, it keeps no record of wrongs. Love does not delight in evil but rejoices with the truth. It always protects, always trusts, always hopes, always perseveres (1 Cor. 13:4-7).

These are words for all relationships at all times. And this love, seen in Jesus and fostered by the Holy Spirit, must control the use of our gifts and abilities.

Other Bible passages that speak about the gifts of the Spirit and how to use them are: Rom. 12:1-8, Eph. 4:11-16 and 1 Peter 4:10-11.

Notice, for instance, how Ephesians 4 teaches the virtually revolutionary truth that the role of church pastors is not to do all the work themselves but to equip the people (mainly through Bible teaching) to do the work using their Spirit-given gifts (Eph. 4:11-13). Many churches would be radically challenged and changed by this teaching, as in many churches most of the work is done by just one or a few people. Too many are content to be no more than passengers, seeking to be served more than to serve. The church is supposed to be more like a team where each player plays a part, with the pastor as the coach.

Action points:

- Never forget that the abilities that we have received from the Holy Spirit are not to be used purely for personal satisfaction, or to make us look good. Always keep in mind their double purpose – the glory of Jesus and the good of others. Then you won't go far wrong.

- Aim to discover the gifts/abilities he has given you and help others do the same. Then play to your strengths in the church.

  Ask yourself, what am I good at and what do I enjoy? Ask other Christians, especially experienced Christians, what they think you are good at. This is often a good way to discover your gifts from the Holy Spirit.

- Look also at the needs of your local church. Since the Holy Spirit is Lord, he may have placed you there to fill these needs or some gap in its services.

  Now offer your services to your church, and to its Lord, fulfilling the potential he has given you.

- At all times, prayerfully depend on the Holy Spirit for, according to 1 Peter 4:11, Christian gifts need to be used 'with the strength God provides'.

Each one should use whatever gift he has received to serve others, faithfully administering God's grace in its various forms. If anyone speaks, he should do it as one speaking the very words of God. If anyone serves, he should do it with the strength God provides, so that in all things God may be praised through Jesus Christ. To him be the glory and the power for ever and ever. Amen (1 Peter 4:10-11).

10
The Guarantee
(of a great future)

It's always good to have a guarantee – that some expectation or commitment will be fulfilled – and not just be left with some vague hope. This is especially true when the promises are great – and there are no greater promises than those made to us in the Bible which Peter describes as 'very great and precious promises' (2 Peter 1:4).

And with these promises, the good news is that God has given us a guarantee.

The Holy Spirit is 'God's guarantee that he will give us the inheritance he promised' (Eph. 1:14; New Living Translation).

Here and in at least two other places in the Bible, Paul speaks clearly of the Holy Spirit as the Christian's guarantee of a great future beyond this life (2 Cor. 1:22 and 5:5; Rom. 5:5 and 8:23 contain a similar thought).

He is like a deposit, a down-payment, guaranteeing that the promised full and glorious inheritance will one day materialize.

Even more, he is actually a foretaste of that future ('the firstfruits of the Spirit', Rom. 8:23). This means that by him we already experience a little of that life and world to come – rather like a television preview of a new blockbuster film or a tasty sample you might be offered in a supermarket (I rarely miss them!) If you're into video games, it's like a trial game or a demo – just a taster intended to make you want the whole thing. So, for all the good we have already experienced in knowing Jesus, it is only a fraction of all that is to come, just a bunch of grapes ('firstfruits') compared with a whole harvest-load of them.

The long-term future of a Christian is truly awesome. I've often thought that when I am speaking about heaven, I do not need to make any qualifications, as we always have to do with even the best things on earth. I never need to say, 'but there is this downside...' There are no downsides to mention, there are only upsides in heaven!

We can hardly imagine how good it will be. 'No eye has seen, no ear has heard, no mind has conceived what God has prepared for those who love him' (1 Cor. 2:9). Though we do have wonderful revelation in Jesus by his Spirit (v10) we may still say of this future glory, *you ain't seen nothin' yet!*

Of course, the popular view of heaven is very different – one of endless boredom. One of the 'Peanuts' cartoons reflects this view:

> Lucy (in class): I wonder if they have fractions in heaven...
> Peppermint Patty (at desk behind Lucy): no fractions, sir... no decimals either
> Lucy: how about commas?
> Peppermint Patty: there have to be commas, sir... we can't avoid them
> Lucy: eternity's going to be longer than I thought...

This could not be further from the truth.

Typically, the word used by the Bible to sum up this future is the word 'glory' (e.g. Rom. 8:18). It conveys a whole range of exciting thoughts including splendour, light, beauty and something that makes an impression on us like nothing else does ('weight of glory' in 2 Cor. 4:17). Our future is more than just bright, it is glorious.

And it is so not because we deserve a great future but because of Jesus Christ and him only – because of his blood, sweat and tears, because of his sacrificial death on the cross and his resurrection to life three days later. In particular 1 Corinthians 15 tells us how our resurrection to glory is guaranteed by Christ's, the first of them all.

So now, through the redemption of Christ and by the renewing power of the Holy Spirit, we can look forward to a whole new world characterized by the total absence of every kind of evil (sin, sorrow, suffering), and the total presence of God and every kind of good.

> And I heard a loud voice from the throne saying, "Now the dwelling of God is with men, and he will live with them. They will be his people, and God himself will be with them and be their God. He will wipe every tear from their eyes. There will be no more death or mourning or crying or pain, for the old order of things has passed away." He who was seated on the throne said, "I am making everything new!" Then he said, "Write this down, for these words are trustworthy and true" (Rev. 21:3-5).

There will be a whole new world with a whole new order, and all so very good. Read Revelation 21 and 22, the Bible's finale, for a thrilling vision of the future in richly symbolic language (where the holy city is symbolic of the bride of Christ, the church, the people of God).

But is this little more than a fairy tale? Or at least just wishful thinking, like so many things in life? Perhaps it is just a hustle like the motto on the TV programme 'The Real Hustle': 'If it sounds too good to be true, it probably is.'

Yes, it sounds too good to be true. And yet it is true! It is a dream that will come true. It is not just wishful thinking, a delusion or a con – because God gives us a double guarantee.

The first guarantee is the (real, historical) resurrection of Jesus Christ from the dead as our forerunner. See the great resurrection chapter 1 Corinthians 15, where Christ's resurrection guarantees ours if we are connected to him through faith.

The second is the gift of the Holy Spirit in the Christian's heart and life (Eph. 1:14; and compare Rom. 5:5), pouring God's love into our experience.

This double guarantee gives us strong confidence and sure hope for the future. It helps us to persevere through the problems of today as we look forward to the pleasures of tomorrow: 'you will fill me with joy in your presence, with eternal pleasures at your right hand' (Ps.16:11).

19th century preacher Charles Spurgeon once said, truly and helpfully, that worry does not empty tomorrow of its sorrows (or anticipated troubles), it only empties today of its strength. Hope, Christian hope, really has the opposite effect – it provides fresh strength today through the anticipation of the glories of tomorrow, the endless tomorrows of the world to come.

Action points:

> We must simply learn to look forward to this future more than anything – our next holiday or even our wedding day, first child or retirement. It is by far the best thing that will ever happen to us and it will last forever. We often say, in this life and world, 'all good things must come to an end.' But in the world to come, good things (unimaginably good things) will last for ever, they will never end nor will there be any disappointment (as we so often experience now).

> 'Now at last they were beginning Chapter One of the Great Story which no one on earth has read: which goes on for ever: in which every chapter is better than the one before' (Lewis, p.212).

The Bible is continually encouraging us to look forward to the bright future lined up for us because of Jesus and all he has done. Peter, for example, writes: 'in keeping with his promise we are looking forward to a new heaven and a new earth, the home of righteousness' (2 Peter 3:13). Look forward to a whole new world, in fact a new universe, a place where everything, and everyone, will be right and good and happy forever!

'Each day should find us like children looking forward to their holidays, who get packed up and ready to go for a long time in advance' (Packer, KC, p.194). So that, rather like the name of a television holiday programme, we say to ourselves in the depths of our hearts, 'I was wish I was there!'

As you do so you can be sure that the Holy Spirit will give you his full support since he himself is (or gives) a taster of that future. In this again, as in other ways, we are to 'keep in step with the Spirit' (Gal. 5:25) – follow his agenda, receive his support.

> - Be sure of your Christian hope. We don't have to be uncertain and doubtful or even vaguely hopeful. Christian hope is not like a weather forecast. It is not of the 'hope-so' variety ('I hope it doesn't rain today'), but a confident expectation about the future. God has given us his double, perhaps we may say treble, guarantee – in the promise of God, in the resurrection of Jesus Christ from the dead and in the gift of the Holy Spirit who lives in all Christians. A treble and Trinitarian guarantee from the Father, Son and Holy Spirit! It doesn't get more secure than that.

So we can be 'sure of what we hope for and certain of what we do not see' (Heb. 11:1) – which has always been a feature of Christians' faith, as Hebrews 11 shows us so clearly.

➤ 'So we fix our eyes not on what is seen, but on what is unseen. For what is seen is temporary, but what is unseen is eternal' (2 Cor. 4:18).

Focus on the future – invisible now but certain and everlasting – not on the present which is merely a passing parade. The older I become the more I find myself looking back to the past with nostalgia, sometimes an unhelpful nostalgia. However, the future is far more interesting and exciting. For believers, life is not all behind us (as we may think as we grow older), it is all in front of us – the resurrection life. The best is yet to come!

Therefore, let us learn from the focused aspiration of the apostle Paul:

'One thing I do: Forgetting what is behind and straining toward what is ahead, I press on toward the goal to win the prize for which God has called me heavenward in Christ Jesus' (Phil. 3:13-14).

➤ Praise God!

> 'Praise be to the God and Father of our Lord Jesus Christ! In his great mercy he has given us new birth into a living hope through the resurrection of Jesus Christ from the dead, and into an inheritance that can never perish, spoil

or fade – kept in heaven for you...' (1 Peter 1:3-4).

In all our thinking about God, about Jesus Christ, about the Holy Spirit, there should always be a melody of praise in our hearts for, in one of my favourite quotations outside the Bible, 'theology [thinking about God] is for doxology and devotion: the praise of God and the practice of godliness' (Packer, CT, p.xii).

And finally, a prayer to the three-in-one God that is often used to conclude church services and always seems to be in season:

'May the grace of the Lord Jesus Christ, and the love of God, and the fellowship of the Holy Spirit be with you all' (2 Cor.13:14).

Amen!

Appendix

John Calvin: the theologian of the Holy Spirit

You will have noticed the name John Calvin cropping up a number of times in the foregoing pages. That is because he had a formidable mind for understanding the Bible – and he still speaks through his writings today. These writings contain frequent references to the many-sided activity of the Holy Spirit in creation and redemption. They earned Calvin the title, 'the theologian of the Holy Spirit', because 'for the first time in the history of the Church, the doctrine of the Holy Spirit comes to its rights ... above everything else, it is the sense of the sovereign working of salvation by the almighty power of the Holy Spirit which characterizes all Calvin's thought of God' (Warfield, pp.485-7).

Following are a series of further quotations from Calvin on the Holy Spirit mostly taken from his major work, *The Institutes of the Christian Religion*, plus some from other sources about Calvin's understanding. It is hoped that these will further enrich your understanding of who the Holy Spirit is and what he does...

The Father, Son and Holy Spirit

> God also designates himself by another special mark to distinguish himself more precisely from idols. For he so proclaims himself the sole God as to offer himself to be contemplated clearly in three persons. Unless we grasp these, only the bare and empty name of God flits about in our brains, to the exclusion of the true God (Inst. 1.13.2).

'The tripersonality of God is conceived by Calvin, therefore, not as something added to the complete idea of God, or as something into which God develops in the process of His existing, but as something which enters into the very idea of God, without which He cannot be conceived in the truth of His being' (Warfield, p.191).

> I cannot think of the one without quickly being encircled by the splendour of the three; nor can I discern the three without being immediately carried back to the one (Inst. 1.13.17).

We have earlier quoted this but it is well worth repeating as it is fair to state that Calvin's thinking runs along these very Trinitarian lines, back and forth from the one being to the three persons and from the three to the one. This is a quotation from a very early Christian (and Trinitarian) thinker known as Gregory of Nazianzus. Calvin wrote that it 'vastly delights' him:

> When we name Father, Son and Spirit, we are not fashioning three gods. But the Scripture and the very experience of piety [the experience of Christian living] shows us, in the very simple essence of God, God the Father, his Son, and his Spirit, in such a way

> that our intellect cannot conceive the Father without comprehending at the same time the Son (in whom brightly shines the vivid image of the Father) and the Spirit (in whom appear power and virtue of the Father) (Calvin, IF, p.46).

As we have earlier said, Calvin finds this reality of the three-in-one God not only in the Bible but also in Christian experience itself.

> Here, indeed, if anywhere in the secret mysteries of Scripture, we ought to play the philosopher soberly and with great moderation; let us use great caution that neither our thoughts nor our speech go beyond the limits to which the Word of God itself extends. For how can the human mind measure off the measureless essence of God according to its own little measure...? (Inst. 1.13.21).

The Trinity is a great mystery and we should not be at all surprised that God is beyond our understanding.

> To the Father is attributed the beginning of activity, and the fountain and wellspring of all things; to the Son, wisdom, counsel and the ordered disposition of all things; but to the Spirit is assigned the power and efficacy of that activity (Inst. 1.13.18).

The giver of life

> It is the Spirit who, everywhere diffused, sustains all things, causes them to grow, and quickens them

> in heaven and earth ... in transfusing into all things his energy, and breathing into them essence, life, movement, he is indeed plainly divine (1.13.14).

> We stand or fall according to the will of God. We continue to live, so long as he sustains us by his power; but no sooner does he withdraw his life-giving spirit than we die ... the world is daily 'renewed', because 'God sends forth his spirit' ... God sends forth that spirit which remains with him whither he pleases; and as soon as he has sent it forth, all things are created (Calvin, *Joshua and the Psalms*).

The impersonal language above can be explained by the thought that it is God the Holy Spirit who sends forth the spirit of life to sustain and renew creation. Calvin is commentating on Ps. 104:29 here.

> The beauty of the universe (which we now perceive) owes its strength and preservation to the power of the Spirit (Inst. 1.13.14).

> He sustains, nourishes and cares for, everything that he has made, even to the least sparrow (Inst. 1.16.1).

> We ought not to forget those most excellent benefits of the divine Spirit, which he distributes to whomever he wills, for the common good of mankind (Inst. 2.2.16).

> He fills, moves and quickens all things by the power of the same Spirit, and does so according to the

> character that he bestowed upon each by the law of creation (Inst. 2.2.16).

The Spirit never works against creation, but always in harmony with it.

The giver of Scripture

> Our religion is distinguished from all others in that the prophets have spoken not of themselves, but as instruments of the Holy Spirit (Calvin's commentary on 2 Tim. 3:16).

> He is the Author of the Scriptures (Inst. 1.9.2).

> It is easy to see that the Sacred Scriptures, which so far surpass all gifts and graces of human endeavour, breathe something divine (Inst. 1.8.1).

> Even if it [the Bible] wins reverence for itself by its own majesty, it seriously affects us only when it is sealed upon our hearts through the Spirit (Inst. 1.7.5).

> He enables those whom he illumines with his Spirit to make such progress as to know his Word and understand it (Calvin in Hartounian ed., *Commentaries*, p.405).

> The same Spirit who made Moses and the prophets certain of their calling, now testifies to our own hearts that he used them as his servants for our instruction

(Calvin's commentary on 2 Tim. 3:16 in Hartounian ed.).

'The great Reformer [Calvin] does not speak of the method of exegesis or the technique of exegesis ... Calvin does these things in a different fashion – deeper, more surprising, more spiritually. When he deals with hermeneutics and the question as to the interpretation of the Bible, then he uses the beautiful expression 'donum interpretationis', the gift of the exegesis of the Scriptures ... Calvin regards the ability to explicate the Scriptures as a gift, something conferred by our highest and only Teacher, Christ' (Floor in van der Walt, p.181).

We might add, to give the fuller sense of Calvin, 'Christ through his Spirit'.

'Exegesis' means the interpretation of the text (of the Bible) so that we read the meaning out of it (and not into it!).

> Therefore, illumined by his power, we believe neither by our own nor by anyone else's judgment that Scripture is from God; but above human judgment we affirm with utter certainty (just as if we were gazing upon the majesty of God himself) that it has flowed to us from the very mouth of God by the ministry of men (Inst. 1.7.5).

We may not feel this way all the time, but Christians have these moments of clarity and certainty – thanks to the Holy Spirit.

> Without the illumination of the Spirit, the Word can do nothing ... we cannot come to Christ unless we be drawn by the Spirit of God (Inst. 3.2.33,34).

> The Word is the instrument by which the Lord dispenses the illumination of the Spirit to believers (Inst. 1.9.3).

'To make the divine authority of the Holy Scripture real to us, we need not a human but a divine testimony ... it is a divine testimony and as such stops all contradiction and silences all doubt' (Kuyper, p.192).

It is the Holy Spirit, the author of the Bible, who gives this 'divine testimony to the Bible' because, as Calvin himself says, 'God alone is a fit witness of himself in his Word.' The Bible is author-authenticated, as if signed by God himself in the front cover!

'Calvin was a man of enthusiastic and sustained study, and Calvin was a man of prayer; '*orare et laborare*' (Floor in van der Walt, p.187-88).

Remember '*orare et laborare*'? It's the essence of good Bible study!

'According to Calvin, Scripture is "the school of the Holy Spirit" or "the school of God" – a metaphor suggesting an ongoing activity of teaching and learning within the context of a living encounter and fellowship' (Rousouw in van der Walt, p.157).

Don't let the word 'school' put you off. This is the best school ever!

> The letter... is dead, and the law of the Lord slays its readers where it is both cut off from Christ's grace (2 Cor. 3:6) and, leaving the heart untouched,

> sounds in the ears alone. But if through the Spirit it is really branded upon hearts, if it shows forth Christ, it is the word of life (Inst. 1.9.3).

'The theological background to Calvin's very strong emphasis on the Holy Spirit with regard to the understanding of the Bible is undoubtedly his faith in the ... corruption of mankind ... Calvin is of the opinion that the greatest impediment towards the understanding of the Scriptures should not be sought in the text or in the language, but in man himself' (Floor in van der Walt, p.186).

The source of power

> Now it is to be noted that the title 'Christ' pertains to these three offices: for we know that under the law prophets as well as priests and kings were anointed with holy oil. Hence the illustrious name of the 'Messiah' was also bestowed upon the promised Mediator... he was anointed by the Spirit (Inst. 2.15.2).

In other words, Jesus Christ performed his work of mediation (between God and ourselves) as prophet, priest and king in the strength of the Holy Spirit.

In fact, Christ:
> ...received anointing, not only for himself that he might carry out the office of teaching, but for his whole body [the church, the people who belong to him] that the power of the Spirit might be present in the continuing preaching of the gospel (Inst. 2.15.2).

Or, for those who would like to try that with a bowl of theological cream: 'the effusion of the Spirit is Christologically grounded' (Weier in Peterson, p.30).

> For the Spirit has chosen Christ as his seat, that from him might abundantly flow the heavenly riches of which we are in such need. The believers stand unconquered through the strength of their king, and his spiritual riches abound in them (Inst. 2.15.5).

Therefore:
> Relying on the power of the Spirit, let us not doubt that we shall always be victorious over the devil, the world, and every kind of harmful thing (Inst. 2.15.4).

Be strong in the Lord!

> God the Father gives us the Holy Spirit for his Son's sake, and yet has bestowed the whole fullness of the Spirit upon the Son to be minister and steward of his liberality (Inst. 3.1.2).

Good Trinitarian thinking!

> Until our minds become intent upon the Spirit, Christ, so to speak, lies idle because we coldly contemplate him as outside ourselves – indeed far from us (Inst. 3.1.3).

Jesus Christ only really becomes real to us through the Holy Spirit.

> The efficient cause of our salvation consists in God the Father's love; the material cause in God the Son's obedience; the instrumental cause in the Spirit's illumination, that is, faith; the final cause, in the glory of God's great generosity (Inst. 3.14.21).

That 'final cause' is by the three-in-one God – Father, Son and Spirit – gloriously generous. Salvation comes to us from the Father, through the Son and by the Spirit.

> The Holy Spirit is the bond by which Christ effectually unites us to himself (Inst. 3.1.1).

Calvin can also refer to 'faith' as this bond because faith is 'the principal work of the Spirit'.

> The Spirit is not only the initiator of faith, but increases it by degrees, until by it he leads us to the Kingdom of heaven (Inst. 3.2.33).

This connection with Christ by the Spirit (through faith) is a wonderful mystery for Calvin, more to be adored and cultivated than understood:

> Let us therefore labour more to feel Christ living in us, than to discover the nature of that communion (Calvin's commentary on Eph. 5:32).

> Faith flows from regeneration as from its source (Calvin's commentary on John 1:13).

> We are reborn into righteousness through his power (Inst. 2.16.13).

> He not only quickens and nourishes us by a general power that is visible both in the human race and in the rest of the living creatures, but he is also the root and seed of heavenly life in us (Inst. 3.1.2).

That is, the Spirit is the giver of life and of new life (through faith in Jesus Christ).

The purifying Spirit

> Regeneration is a renewal of the divine image in us (Inst. 3.17.5).

We become more, not less, human when we become believers in Jesus Christ. 'The effect of the Spirit is to make us truly natural' (Wallace, p.192).

> Who would have such strife in himself but a man who, regenerated by the Spirit of God, bears the remains of his flesh about him (Inst. 2.2.27).

The battle with personal sin only really begins when we are renewed by the Holy Spirit and become Christians.

> The Spirit dispenses a power whereby they [God's people] may gain the upper hand and become victors in the struggle. But sin ceases only to reign; it does not also cease to dwell in them (Inst. 3.3.11).

The process of purification (or sanctification) has begun and can make progress in the power of the Spirit.

> [Faith is] a firm and certain knowledge of God's benevolence toward us, founded upon the truth of the freely given promise in Christ, both revealed to our minds and sealed upon our hearts through the Holy Spirit (Inst. 3.2.7).

> Indeed, the Word of God is like the sun, shining upon all those to whom it is proclaimed, but with no effect among the blind ... it cannot penetrate into our minds unless the Spirit, as the inner teacher, through his illumination makes entry for it (Inst. 3.2.34).

Calvin often speaks of the Holy Spirit as our 'inner teacher', bringing home to our hearts the truth he has inspired in the Bible.

> We cannot come to Christ unless we be drawn by the Spirit of God ... when we are drawn we are lifted up in mind and heart above our understanding (Inst. 3.2.34).

For Calvin, faith does not work against reason but it certainly lifts us above reason. The Holy Spirit elevates believers in a spiritual way into the very presence of Christ at the right hand of God the Father – to receive his grace.

> [Repentance is] a true turning of our life to God, a turning that arises from a pure and earnest fear of him; and it consists in the mortification of our flesh and of the old man [or nature], and in the vivification of the Spirit (Inst. 3.3.5).

This involves more than a change of external actions: 'we require a transformation, not only in the outward works, but in the soul itself' (Inst. 3.3.6). This clearly points in the direction of the Holy Spirit and regeneration.

> This comes to pass when the Spirit of God so imbues our souls, steeped in his holiness, with both new thoughts and feelings, that they can rightly be considered new (Inst. 3.3.8).

Compare this with Philippians 2:12-13 considered earlier.

> They whose consciences, though convinced that what they repudiate and impugn is the Word of God, yet cease not to impugn it – these are said to blaspheme against the Spirit, since they strive against the illumination that is the work of the Holy Spirit (Inst. 3.3.22).

This is the sin against the Holy Spirit and it is dreadfully serious.

> The Christian philosophy bids reason give way to, submit and subject itself to, the Holy Spirit so that the man himself may no longer live but may hear Christ living and reigning within him (Gal. 2:20) (Inst. 3.7.1).

> [On suffering:] By communion with him [through the Spirit] the very sufferings themselves not only become blessed to us but also help much in promoting our salvation (Inst. 3.8.1).

> When they have betaken themselves there [to God's grace] they experience the presence of a divine power [the Holy Spirit] in which they have protection enough and to spare (Inst. 3.8.2).

> When the favour of God breathes upon us [clear reference to the Spirit], every one of these things turns into happiness for us (Inst. 3.8.7).

Calvin is talking about major sufferings like poverty, exile, contempt, prison, disgrace and finally 'death itself the ultimate of all calamities'.

The giver of hope

In the Spirit, we may be at once 'so stabbed with bitterness, [yet] at the same time flooded with spiritual joy' – the hope-filled joy experienced only by believers in times of trouble.

> Shall we, endowed with the light of understanding and above understanding illumined with the Spirit of God, when our very being is at stake, not lift our minds beyond this earthly decay? (Inst. 3.9.5).

In other words, the Spirit helps us to hope. He stirs up hope in our hearts, particularly in times of despair.

> In Scripture the Spirit of God is continually urging us to hope for the resurrection of our flesh (Inst. 3.25.8).

The inspirer of prayer

> God gives us the Spirit as our teacher in prayer, to tell us what is right and temper [moderate] our emotions (Inst. 3.20.5).

The Holy Spirit is the key to real prayer, without him our prayers are nothing.

> The prompting of the Spirit empowers us so to compose prayers as by no means to hinder or hold back our own effort (Inst. 3.20.5).

The Holy Spirit does not pray for us; he empowers us to pray. He does not make us passive in prayer, he makes us active.

'We are invited to see prayer not primarily as a duty required of us, but much more as a gift given to us by the Holy Spirit: God on our side of the relationship' (Smail, p.205).

Calvin goes on to describe prayer, wonderfully, as 'intimate conversation' with God – an intimacy given by the Holy Spirit.

The giver of love, gifts and unity

> They are truly made one since they live together ... in the same Spirit of God (Inst. 4.1.2).

As has earlier been said, Christians do not create their unity, we only have to keep it.

> The saints are gathered into the society of Christ on the principle that whatever benefits God confers on them, they should in turn share with one another. This does not, however, rule out diversity of graces, inasmuch as we know the gifts of the Spirit are distributed variously (Inst. 4.1.3).

The Holy Spirit's diverse gifts are given 'for the common good'.

> The Lord has so divided his manifold graces among men, that no one is content with one thing and with his own gifts, but everyone needs the help and aid of his brother. This, I say, is a bond which God has appointed for preserving fellowship (Calvin quoted by Elbert, p.119).

The diversity of gifting creates a wonderful interdependence amongst the members of a church.

'There is no one so void of gifts in the church of Christ who is not able to contribute something to our benefit' (Milner, p.183).

Everyone has something to offer.

The essential Spirit

On the 'sacraments' (baptism and communion):

> For, first, the Lord teaches and instructs us by his Word. Secondly, he confirms it by the sacraments. Finally, he illumines our minds by the light of his Holy Spirit and opens our hearts for Word and sacraments to enter in, which would otherwise only strike our ears and appear before our eyes, but not at all affect us within (Inst. 4.14.8).

> The sacraments properly fulfil their office only when the Spirit, that inward teacher, comes to them, by

whose power alone hearts are penetrated and affections moved and our souls opened for the sacraments to enter in. If the Spirit be lacking, the sacraments can accomplish nothing more in our minds than the splendour of the sun shining upon blind eyes, or a voice sounding in deaf ears ... a ministry empty and trifling apart from the action of the Spirit, but charged with great effect when the Spirit works within and manifests his power (Inst. 4.14.9).

The Holy Spirit is always the essential. Nothing we do, however religious, is of any use or any value unless he is in it. But when he *is* in it, great things can happen!

***

If you have any questions or comments, feel free to email me: oliver.rice@gmail.com

Additional References:

Apart from the 'Institutes', most of the additional Calvin references have been taken from his biblical commentaries. All other sources are given below:

D.J. Atkinson ed., *New Dictionary of Christian Ethics and Pastoral Theology*, IVP, 1995.

J.M. Boice, *Foundations of the Christian Faith*, IVP, 1986.

J. Calvin, *Instruction in Faith* (1537) (IF), Lutterworth Press, 1949.

P. Elbert, 'Calvin and the Spiritual Gifts' in *Essays on Apostolic Themes,* Hendrickson, 1985.

S. Ferguson, *The Doctrine of the Holy Spirit*, IVP, 1997.

A. Kuyper, *The Work of the Holy Spirit*, Eerdmans, 1956.

C.S. Lewis, *The Last Battle*, Harper Collins, 1956.

D. MacLeod, *The Spirit of Promise*, Christian Focus, 1986.

B.C. Milner, *Calvin's Doctrine of the Church*, E.J. Brill, 1970.

J.I. Packer, *Concise Theology* (CT), IVP, 1993.

J.I. Packer, *Knowing Christianity* (KC), Eagle, 1995.

R.A. Peterson, *Calvin's Doctrine of the Atonement*, Presbyterian and Reformed Publishing Company, 1983.

T. Smail, *The Giving Gift*, Hodder & Stoughton, 1988.

R.S. Wallace, *Calvin's Doctrine of the Christian Life*, Oliver and Boyd, 1959.

B.J. van der Walt, *Calvinus Reformator*, Potchefstroom University, 1982.

B.B. Warfield, *Calvin and Augustine*, The Presbyterian and Reformed Publishing Company, 1956.